KNOWING JESUS

—✦ Foundations of the Faith ✦—

GROUP DIRECTORY

Pass this Directory around and have your Group Members
fill in their names and phone numbers

Name   **Phone**

_____   _____

_____   _____

_____   _____

_____   _____

_____   _____

_____   _____

_____   _____

_____   _____

_____   _____

_____   _____

_____   _____

_____   _____

_____   _____

_____   _____

KNOWING JESUS

✦ Foundations of the Faith ✦

EDITING AND PRODUCTION TEAM:

James F. Couch, Jr., Lyman Coleman, Sharon Penington, Gregory C. Benoit,
Christopher Werner, Matthew Lockhart, Richard Peace, Andrew Sloan,
Cathy Tardif, Scott Lee, Erika Tiepel, Mary Chatfield

SERENDIPITY
HOUSE

NASHVILLE, TENNESSEE

Published by Serendipity House Publishers
Nashville, Tennessee

International Standard Book Number: 1-57494-310-3

ACKNOWLEDGMENTS

Scripture quotations are taken from the Holman Christian Standard Bible,
© Copyright 2000 by Holman Bible Publishers. Used by permission.

Nashville, Tennessee
1-800-525-9563
www.serendipityhouse.com

TABLE OF CONTENTS

Session	Reference	Subject	Page
1	Mark 8:27–36	Messiah	15
2	Mark 4:1–20	Teacher	23
3	Matthew 9:18–34	Healer	31
4	Matthew 4:1–11	Tempted	39
5	Mark 2:13–22; 3:1–6	Revolutionary	47
6	Mark 14:12–26	Redeemer	55
7	Ephesians 2:11–22	Reconciler	63

CORE VALUES

Community: The purpose of this curriculum is to build community within the body of believers around Jesus Christ.

Group Process: To build community, the curriculum must be designed to take a group through a step-by-step process of sharing your story with one another.

Interactive Bible Study: To share your "story," the approach to Scripture in the curriculum needs to be open-ended and right brain—to "level the playing field" and encourage everyone to share.

Developmental Stages: To provide a healthy program throughout the four stages of the life cycle of a group, the curriculum needs to offer courses on three levels of commitment: (1) Beginner Level—low-level entry, high structure, to level the playing field; (2) Growth Level—deeper Bible study, flexible structure, to encourage group accountability; (3) Discipleship Level—in-depth Bible study, open structure, to move the group into high gear.

Target Audiences: To build community throughout the culture of the church, the curriculum needs to be flexible, adaptable and transferable into the structure of the average church.

Mission: To expand the kingdom of God one person at a time by filling the "empty chair." (We add an extra chair to each group session to remind us of our mission.)

INTRODUCTION

EACH HEALTHY SMALL GROUP WILL MOVE THROUGH VARIOUS STAGES AS IT MATURES.

Multiply Stage: The group begins the multiplication process. Members pray about their involvement in new groups. The "new" groups begin the life cycle again with the Birth Stage.

Birth Stage: This is the time in which group members form relationships and begin to develop community. The group will spend more time in ice-breaker exercises, relational Bible study and covenant building.

Develop Stage: The inductive Bible study deepens while the group members discover and develop gifts and skills. The group explores ways to invite their neighbors and coworkers to group meetings.

Growth Stage: Here the group begins to care for one another as it learns to apply what they learn through Bible study, worship and prayer.

 **Subgrouping:** If you have nine or more people at a meeting, Serendipity recommends you divide into subgroups of 3–6 for the Bible study. Ask one person to be the leader of each subgroup and to follow the directions for the Bible study. After 30 minutes, the Group Leader will call "time" and ask all subgroups to come together for the Caring Time.

EACH GROUP MEETING SHOULD INCLUDE ALL PARTS OF THE "THREE-PART AGENDA."

 Ice-Breaker: Fun, history-giving questions are designed to warm the group and to build understanding about the other group members. You can choose to use all of the Ice-Breaker questions, especially if there is a new group member that will need help in feeling comfortable with the group.

One of the purposes of this book is to begin a group. Therefore, getting to know one another and bonding together are esstential to the success of this course. The goal is to get acquainted during the Ice-Breaker part of each group session.

 Bible Study: The heart of each meeting is the reading and examination of the Bible. The questions are open, discover questions that lead to further inquiry. Reference notes are provided to give everyone a "level playing field." The emphasis is on understanding what the Bible says and applying the truth to real life. The questions for each session build. There is always at least one "going deeper" question provided. You should always leave time for the last of the "questions for interaction." Should you choose, you can use the optional "going deeper" question to satisfy the desire for the challenging questions in groups that have been together for a while.

To help bond together as a group, it is important for everyone to participate in the Bible Study. There are no right or wrong answers to the questions. The group members should strive to make all of the other group members feel comfortable during the Bible Study time. Because we all have differing levels of biblical knowledge, it is essential that we appreciate the personal context from which answers are given. We don't have to know much about Scripture to bring our own perspectives on the truths contained in the Scriptures. It is vital to keep encouraging all group members to share what they are observing as we work through these important Bible passages.

 Caring Time: All study should point us to actions. Each session ends with prayer and direction in caring for the needs of the group members. You can choose between several questions. You should always pray for the "empty chair." Who do you know that could fill that void in your group?

Small groups help the larger body of Christ in many ways: caring for individuals, holding one another up in prayer, providing emotional support and in bringing new people into the body through filling the empty chair. Each week it is important to remember to pray for those who God would bring to fill your empty chair.

Sharing Your Story: These sessions are designed for members to share a little of their personal lives each time. Through a number of special techniques, each member is encouraged to move from low risk, less personal sharing to higher risk responses. This helps develop the sense of community and facilitates caregiving.

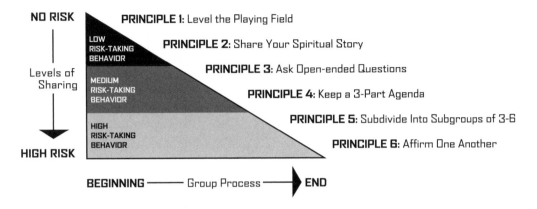

Group Covenant: A group covenant is a "contract" that spells out your expectations and the ground rules for your group. It's very important that your group discuss these issues—preferably as part of the first session.

GROUND RULES:

- *Priority:* While you are in the group, you give the group meeting priority.

- *Participation:* Everyone participates and no one dominates.

- *Respect:* Everyone is given the right to their own opinion and all questions are encouraged and respected.

- *Confidentiality:* Anything that is said in the meeting is never repeated outside the meeting.

- *Empty Chair:* The group stays open to new people at every meeting.

- *Support:* Permission is given to call upon each other in time of need—even in the middle of the night.

- *Advice Giving:* Unsolicited advice is not allowed.

- *Mission:* We agree to do everything in our power to start a new group as our mission.

GOALS:

- The time and place this group is going to meet is_____.

- Refreshments are _____ responsibility.

- Child care is _____ responsibility.

- This group will meet until _____ at which time we will decide to split into new groups or continue our sessions together.

- Our primary purpose for meeting is _____.

OUR SMALL GROUP COVENANT

1. The facilitator for this group is _____.

2. The apprentice facilitator for this group is _____.

3. This group will meet from _____ to _____ on _____.

4. This group will normally meet at _____.

5. Child care will be arranged by _____.

6. Refreshments will be coordinated by _____.

7. Our primary purpose for meeting is _____.

8. Our secondary purpose for meeting is _____.

9. We all agree to follow the ground rules listed below:

    a. This meeting will be given priority in our schedules.

    b. Everyone will participate in each meeting and no one will dominate a meeting.

    c. Each has a right to one's own opinion and all questions will be respected.

    d. Everything that is said in group meetings is never to be repeated outside of the meeting.

    e. This group will be open to new people at every meeting.

    f. Permission is given for all to call on each other in time of need.

    g. Unsolicited advice is not allowed.

    h. We agree to fill the empty chair and work toward starting new groups.

10. We are to hold one another accountable to meet any commitments mutually agreed upon by this group.

I agree to all of the above _____ date _____

FELT NEED SURVEY

Rank the following factors in order of importance to you with 1 being the highest and 5 being the lowest:

_____ The passage of Scripture that is being studied.
_____ The topic or issue that is being discussed.
_____ The affinity of group members (age, vocation, interest).
_____ The mission of the group (service projects, evangelism, starting groups).
_____ Personal encouragement.

Rank the following spiritual development needs in order of interest to you with 1 being the highest and 5 being the lowest:

_____ Learning how to become a follower of Christ.
_____ Gaining a basic understanding of the truths of the faith.
_____ Improving my disciplines of devotion, prayer, reading Scripture.
_____ Gaining a better knowledge of what is in the Bible.
_____ Applying the truths of Scripture to my life.

Of the various studies below, check the appropriate boxes that indicate: if you would be interested in studying for your personal needs (P), you think would be helpful for your group (G), or you have friends that are not in the group that would come to a study of this subject (F).

	P	G	F
Growing in Christ Series (7-week studies)			
Keeping Your Cool: Dealing With Stress	☐	☐	☐
Personal Audit: Assessing Your Life	☐	☐	☐
Seasons of Growth: Stages of Marriage	☐	☐	☐
Checking Your Moral Compass: Personal Morals	☐	☐	☐
Women of Faith (8 weeks)	☐	☐	☐
Men of Faith	☐	☐	☐
Becoming a Disciple (7-week studies)			
Discovering God's Will	☐	☐	☐
Time for a Checkup	☐	☐	☐
Learning to Love	☐	☐	☐
Foundations of the Faith (7-week studies)			
Knowing Jesus	☐	☐	☐
Foundational Truths	☐	☐	☐
Understanding the Savior (13-week studies)			
Mark 1–8: Jesus, the Early Years	☐	☐	☐
Mark 8–16: Jesus, the Final Days	☐	☐	☐
John 1–11: God in the Flesh	☐	☐	☐

	P	G	F
John 12–21: The Passion of the Son	☐	☐	☐
The Miracles of Jesus	☐	☐	☐
The Life of Christ	☐	☐	☐
The Parables of Jesus	☐	☐	☐
The Sermon on the Mount: Jesus, the Teacher	☐	☐	☐

The Message of Paul

Romans 1–7: Who We Really Are (13 weeks)	☐	☐	☐
Romans 8–16: Being a Part of God's Plan (13 weeks)	☐	☐	☐
1 Corinthians: Taking on Tough Issues (13 weeks)	☐	☐	☐
Galatians: Living by Grace (13 weeks)	☐	☐	☐
Ephesians: Together in Christ (12 weeks)	☐	☐	☐
Philippians: Running the Race (7 weeks)	☐	☐	☐

Words of Faith

Acts 1–14: The Church on Fire (13 weeks)	☐	☐	☐
Acts 15–28: The Irrepressible Witness (13 weeks)	☐	☐	☐
Hebrews: Jesus Through the Eyes of Hebrew Faith (13 weeks)	☐	☐	☐
James: Faith at Work (12 weeks)	☐	☐	☐
1 Peter: Staying the Course (10 weeks)	☐	☐	☐
1 John: Walking in the Light (11 weeks)	☐	☐	☐
Revelation 1–12: End of Time (13 weeks)	☐	☐	☐
Revelation 13–22: The New Jerusalem (13 weeks)	☐	☐	☐

301 Bible Studies with Homework Assignments (13-week studies)

Ephesians: Our Riches in Christ	☐	☐	☐
James: Walking the Talk	☐	☐	☐
Life of Christ: Behold the Man	☐	☐	☐
Miracles: Signs and Wonders	☐	☐	☐
Parables: Virtual Reality	☐	☐	☐
Philippians: Joy Under Stress	☐	☐	☐
Sermon on the Mount: Examining Your Life	☐	☐	☐
1 John: The Test of Faith	☐	☐	☐

Felt Need Series (7-week studies)

Stress Management: Finding the Balance	☐	☐	☐
12 Steps: The Path to Wholeness	☐	☐	☐
Divorce Recovery: Picking Up the Pieces	☐	☐	☐
Parenting Adolescents: Easing the Way to Adulthood	☐	☐	☐
Blended Families: Yours, Mine, Ours	☐	☐	☐
Dealing with Grief and Loss: Hope in the Midst of Pain	☐	☐	☐
Healthy Relationships: Living Within Defined Boundaries	☐	☐	☐
Marriage Enrichment: Making a Good Marriage Better	☐	☐	☐

MESSIAH

SCRIPTURE   MARK 8 : 27 – 36

WELCOME

WELCOME TO THIS STUDY ON THE PERSON OF JESUS CHRIST. JESUS HAS HAD A PROFOUND INFLUENCE ON THE WORLD—MORE SO THAN ANY OTHER PERSON. HIS STORY IS A MAJOR THEME OF WESTERN HISTORY. IN FACT, THE EVENTS OF HISTORY ARE MEASURED BY WHETHER THEY HAPPENED BEFORE HIS BIRTH (B.C.) OR AFTER (A.D.).

Despite Jesus' great influence, there is still at best a sense of mystery surrounding him, and at worst a great misunderstanding. Who was Jesus? What was he like? Although they are not a valid source of information, modern theatrical representations reflect the wrong thinking about Jesus that is prominent in our society. *The Greatest Story Ever Told* (1965) pictures Jesus as an otherworldly figure, somewhat oddly intersecting with the world as we know it. He speaks King James English, while everyone else talks like an American. In Jesus Christ Superstar (1973), Jesus is a discontented hippie, prone to strong emotions and outbursts of passion. The film *Jesus* (1979) presents a very mild, likable Jesus with a kind of "father knows best" demeanor. Franco Zeffirelli, director of the popular 1983 film *Jesus of Nazareth*, was committed to portraying Jesus according to biblical accounts. In sharp contrast, *The Last Temptation of Christ* (1988) pictures Jesus as a tortured soul prone to severe bouts of self-doubt and self-hatred. Everyone has some image of Jesus, though most are distorted, through which they try to understand him. If we are not careful we end up with a Jesus who is more a product of our culture than of Scripture.

In the gospel of Mark, Jesus asks his disciples who people believe he is and they respond, "John the Baptist; others, Elijah; still others, one of the prophets." But then Jesus asks the ultimate question: "But you, who do you say that I am?" This is the most important question we need to answer for ourselves. It is a question we will look at in our first study, and which we will keep in mind throughout our study of getting to know Jesus better. Do we have a distorted worldly view or do we know the Jesus of the Bible?

ICE-BREAKER   15 min

CONNECT WITH YOUR GROUP

LEADER

Open with a word of prayer, asking for God's blessing as you study his Word and seek to grow together as a group. Select two or three of the Ice-Breaker questions to help get people started talking together comfortably.

Many of us search long and hard to discover who we are and what our purpose is in life. As we begin this study together, help others get to know you better by sharing some thoughts about who you are.

1.　Where were you born, and what do you know about the circumstances surrounding your birth?

2.　Which of the following experiences has taught you the most about who you are?
　• My marriage.
　• A divorce.
　• A new job.
　• A health crisis.
　• The death of a loved one.
　• Living away from home.
　• Other _____.

3.　If your friends or family were asked what one word best describes you, what would they say?

BIBLE STUDY　　　　　30 min

READ SCRIPTURE AND DISCUSS

LEADER

Select a member of the group ahead of time to read aloud the Scripture passage. Then discuss the Questions for Interaction, dividing into subgroups of three to six. Be sure to save at least 15 minutes at the end for the Caring Time.

This is an important passage in Mark's gospel, as Jesus is revealed to be the long-awaited Messiah. Peter's ideas about the Messiah, however, reflect the popular expectations that the Messiah would be a political, military hero. Read Mark 8:27–36, and note Jesus' response to Peter.

Peter's Confession of Christ

²⁷ Jesus went out with His disciples to the villages of Caesarea Philippi. And on the road He asked His disciples, "Who do people say that I am?"

²⁸And they answered Him, "John the Baptist; others, Elijah; still others, one of the prophets."

²⁹"But you," He asked them again, "who do you say that I am?"
Peter answered Him, "You are the Messiah!"

³⁰And He strictly warned them to tell no one about Him.

³¹Then He began to teach them that the Son of Man must suffer many things, and be rejected by the elders, the chief priests, and the scribes, be killed, and rise after three days. ³²And He was openly talking about this. So Peter took Him aside and began to rebuke Him.

³³But turning around and looking at His disciples, He rebuked Peter and said, "Get behind Me, Satan, because you're not thinking about God's concerns, but man's!"

³⁴Summoning the crowd along with His disciples, He said to them, "If anyone wants to be My follower, he must deny himself, take up his cross, and follow Me. ³⁵For whoever wants to save his life will lose it, but whoever loses his life because of Me and the gospel will save it. ³⁶For what does it benefit a man to gain the whole world yet lose his life?

Mark 8:27–36

QUESTIONS FOR INTERACTION

LEADER

Refer to the Summary and Study Notes at the end of this session as needed. If 30 minutes is not enough time to answer all of the following questions, conclude the Bible Study by answering questions 6 and 7.

1. Why do you think Jesus asked his disciples who people said he was?

2. If you asked the typical person today, "Who is Jesus Christ?" what answer would they give?
    • The founder of a religion.
    • The greatest man who ever lived.
    • The Son of God.
    • A spiritual philosopher and teacher.
    • A social revolutionary.
    • My Lord and Savior.
    • Other _____.

3. What is your answer to the question, "Who is Jesus Christ?" Why?

4. Peter states that Jesus is the Christ, or the Messiah. What does Jesus say that the Messiah came to do?

5. Why do you think that Peter rebukes Jesus? Why does Jesus rebuke him?

6. The central affirmation of the early church was "Jesus is Lord," while everyone else was saying, "Caesar is Lord." What "gods" compete with your allegiance to Christ?
   • Power and influence.
   • My friends or family.
   • Pleasure and fun.
   • Wealth and possessions.
   • My career.
   • My reputation.
   • Other _____.

7. What needs to be the next step in your spiritual life?
   • To say "no" to the competing allegiances in my life.
   • To correct my misconceptions of who Jesus is.
   • To do some work on the "basics"—prayer, Bible reading, etc.
   • To confess my faith publicly, as Peter did.
   • To "lose my life" and turn from self-focus to Christ-focus.
   • To be more involved with church life, small groups, etc.
   • Other _____.

GOING DEEPER

If your group has time and/or wants a challenge, go on to this question.

8. Why must Jesus' followers "deny" themselves? How do verses 34 and 35 relate to Jesus' own mission?

CARING TIME   15 min

APPLY THE LESSON AND PRAY FOR ONE ANOTHER

LEADER

Take some extra time in this first session to go over the group covenant and ground rules found at the beginning of this book. At the close, pass around your books and have everyone sign the Group Directory.

This very important time is for developing and expressing your concern for each other as group members by praying for one another.

1.   Agree on the group covenant and ground rules found in the introductory pages.

2.   How can the group help you to answer the question, "Who is Jesus?"

3.   Share any other prayer requests and then close in prayer. Pray specifically for God to bring someone into your life next week to fill the empty chair.

NEXT WEEK

Today we began to discover who Jesus is by looking at how the disciples responded to Jesus' question, "But you, who do you say that I am?" Peter understood that Jesus was the Messiah they had been waiting for, but didn't understand how Jesus would have to suffer and die for the sins of all humanity. In the coming week, read the Bible and pray that God will show you more of the real Jesus. Next week we will focus on Jesus' role as a teacher and look at how we respond to his teachings.

NOTES ON MARK 8:27 - 36

Summary: This is a pivotal passage in the gospel of Mark. The disciples declare (through Peter, who seems to have become their spokesman) that in contrast to the crowds, they recognize who Jesus is. He is the long-expected Messiah. To be sure, they have the wrong idea about the nature and role of the Messiah. But at least they have grasped accurately that Jesus is not just an exceptional rabbi, nor just a wonder-worker.

8:27 *Caesarea Philippi.* A beautiful city on the slopes of Mount Hermon, 25 miles north of Bethsaida. It had been a center of Baal worship, and was said to be the birthplace of the god Pan. It was also the place where the River Jordan began. At the time when Jesus and his disciples visited there, up on the hill was a gleaming, white marble temple dedicated to the godhead of Caesar. It is fitting that in this place with rich associations to the religions of the world, Jesus, the Galilean, asks his disciples if they understand that he is the Anointed One sent by God.

8:29 *who do you say that I am?* This is the crucial question in Mark's gospel. By it the author forces his readers to consider how they will answer the question as well. *You are the Messiah.* Peter correctly identifies him as the Messiah. "Christ" is the Greek term for "Messiah" (which is a Hebrew word). In the context of Jewish thought, this meant the prophesied future king of Israel who would deliver Israel from bondage into an era of freedom, power, influence and prosperity.

8:30 *to tell no one.* Jesus urges them to be silent about what they know. The problem is that although they know that he is the Messiah, they do not yet know what kind of Messiah he is. Like the blind man, the disciples have received the "first touch" of healing. Their spiritual blindness, which thus far prevented them from understanding Jesus, is beginning to be healed but they are not yet totally restored to full sight as the next incident shows (8:31–33).

8:31 To predict one's death is rare, but not unknown. However, to predict that one will rise from the dead is startling. No wonder the disciples had trouble taking in what he was saying. The repetition three times of this prediction of death and resurrection draws attention to its central importance in understanding who Jesus is. *Son of Man.* This appears in Daniel 7:13 and it is a clear reference to the Messiah. *rejected by the elders, the chief priests, and the scribes.* These three groups made up the Sanhedrin, the ruling Jewish body. Jesus is predicting that he will be officially rejected by Israel (Mark 14:55). *be killed.* The death of the Messiah at the hands of Israel's official governing body played no part in popular ideas about the Messiah. This was a startling, incomprehensible announcement. For Jesus, his death was mandated by a divine necessity.

8:32 *rebuke.* Peter, who moments before identifies Jesus as the Messiah, is startled by his teaching that the Messiah will suffer, be rejected, killed and then rise from the dead. He felt compelled to take Jesus aside and urge him to stop this line of teaching. The word "rebuke" is the same one used to describe the silencing of demons.

8:33 *Get behind Me, Satan.* While Peter is not Satan, his words reflect the goals of Satan.

8:34 *the crowd.* Everyone who wishes to follow Jesus is intended to hear his message. While the miracles might have made it appear that the kingdom of God simply meant fulfillment and joy, Jesus makes it clear that the way to the kingdom involves self-denial and sacrifice. Mark appears to have especially directed these words to the situation faced by the original recipients of the Gospel, the Christians in Rome who were in fact suffering for the sake of Jesus during the persecution under Nero. *follow Me.* Discipleship is a matter of following in the ways of one's teacher. *deny himself / take up his cross / follow Me.* To "take up a cross" was something done only by a person sentenced to death by crucifixion, a reality that had faced some of the comrades of Mark's readers who had been executed by Nero. This stark image points out that to be a follower of Jesus means that loyalty to him must precede all desires and ambitions, including the natural desire for self-preservation. Like Jesus, his followers are to single-mindedly pursue God's way even when it means suffering and death.

8:35 *save his life.* The image is of a trial in which one is called upon to renounce Jesus in order to live. This would have immediate application to the Christians in Rome who were pressed with the decision of considering whether to affirm their loyalty to Jesus and face the persecution of the state or deny their association with Jesus and be allowed to live.

◆ S E S S I O N   2 ◆

TEACHER

SCRIPTURE   MARK 4:1–20

◆ Foundations of the Faith ◆

LAST WEEK

IN LAST WEEK'S SESSION, WE BEGAN TO EXPLORE THE COMPLEX ISSUE OF JESUS' IDENTITY AND PURPOSE. WE FOCUSED ON HIS ROLE AS THE MESSIAH, THE LONG-AWAITED SAVIOR THAT WAS SENT BY GOD TO FREE HIS PEOPLE FROM SIN AND DEATH. THIS WEEK WE WILL CONSIDER JESUS' ROLE AS A TEACHER, AND LOOK AT THE MANY WAYS THAT PEOPLE RESPOND TO HIS TEACHINGS. WE WILL ALSO EVALUATE HOW WE EACH PERSONALLY TRY TO FOLLOW JESUS' TEACHINGS.

ICE-BREAKER   15 min

CONNECT WITH YOUR GROUP

LEADER

Open with a word of prayer, and then introduce any new group members. Select one, two or all three Ice-Breaker questions to begin the study. Be sure that everyone gets a chance to participate.

Parables are stories that Jesus often used to teach difficult spiritual truths. In picturesque language, he would communicate insights about God, his kingdom and the response expected of those who were listening. Take turns sharing some of your experiences with teaching and learning.

1.   Who is the best teacher you ever had? How did that person influence your life?

2.   If you could teach any subject at the college level, what would it be, and why?
      • Philosophy.
      • Wilderness Survival.
      • Music Theory.
      • Women in Literature.
      • Small Business Management.
      • How to Succeed Without Really Trying.
      • Other _____.

3.   As a child, what was your favorite story or fairy tale, and why?

BIBLE STUDY — 30 min

READ SCRIPTURE AND DISCUSS

LEADER

Ask two group members, selected ahead of time, to read aloud the Scripture passage. Have one member read the part of Mark, the narrator; and the other read the part of Jesus. Then discuss the Questions for Interaction, dividing into subgroups of three to six.

The emphasis of this parable is on the soils. Mark helps the reader to understand the four types of responses to Jesus: two that are negative and two that are positive. However, it becomes clear from the Lord's explanation that only one response will bear fruit for the kingdom. Read Mark 4:1–20, and note what that correct response is.

The Parable of the Sower

Mark: 4 Again He began to teach by the sea, and a very large crowd gathered around Him. So He got into a boat on the sea and sat down, while the whole crowd was on the shore facing the sea. ²He taught them many things in parables, and in His teaching He said to them:

Jesus: ³"Listen! Consider the sower who went out to sow. ⁴As he sowed, this occurred: Some seed fell along the path, and the birds came and ate it up. ⁵Other seed fell on rocky ground where it didn't have much soil, and it sprang up right away, since it didn't have deep soil. ⁶When the sun came up, it was scorched, and since it didn't have a root, it withered. ⁷Other seed fell among thorns, and the thorns came up and choked it, and it didn't produce a crop. ⁸Still others fell on good ground and produced a crop that increased 30, 60, and 100 times what was sown."

Mark: ⁹Then He said,

Jesus: "Anyone who has ears to hear should listen!"

Mark: ¹⁰When He was in private, those who were around Him, along with the Twelve. asked Him about the parables. ¹¹He answered them.

⇜ Foundations of the Faith ⇝

Jesus: "The secret of the kingdom of God has been granted to you, but to those outside, everything comes in parables [12]so that

> they may look and look, yet not perceive;
>
> they may listen and listen, yet not understand;
>
> otherwise, they might turn back—and be forgiven."

Mark: [13]Then He said to them:

Jesus: "Do you not understand this parable? How then will you understand all the parables? [14]The sower sows the word. [15]These are the ones along the path where the word is sown: when they hear, immediately Satan comes and takes away the word sown in them. [16]And these are the ones sown on rocky ground: when they hear the word, immediately they receive it with joy. [17]But they have no root in themselves; they are short-lived. And when affliction or persecution comes because of the word, they stumble immediately. [18]Others are sown among thorns; these are the ones who hear the word, [19]but the worries of this age, the pleasure of wealth, and the desires for other things enter in and choke the word, and it becomes unfruitful. [20]But the ones sown on good ground are those who hear the word, welcome it, and produce a crop: 30, 60, and 100 times what was sown."

Mark 4:1–20

QUESTIONS FOR INTERACTION

LEADER

Refer to the Summary and Study Notes at the end of this session as needed. If 30 minutes is not enough time to answer all of the questions in this section, conclude the Bible Study by answering questions 6 and 7.

1.   What is your initial reaction to this passage?

2.   What does Jesus mean in verse 9, "Anyone who has ears to hear should listen"?

3.   What sort of person might "look and look, yet not perceive" (v. 12) the truth of Jesus' teachings?

4.   According to Jesus, why does God's Word not take root at all in some people (v. 15)?

5.   What do you have right now in your life that gives depth to your "soil" and nurtures your growth?

6.   What are the thorns and rocks in your life that tend to choke out spiritual growth?
      • Pressure from others.
      • Influence of our culture.
      • Lack of commitment or discipline.
      • Parties/alcohol/drugs.
      • Worry about the future or about finances.
      • Church activities.
      • Other _____.

7.   What steps could you take to improve the soil of your spiritual life?

GOING DEEPER

If your group has time and/or wants a challenge, go on to this question.

8.   In verse 12, Jesus is quoting from Isaiah 6:9–10 (see notes). What does he mean here? Does God trick people into not believing him?

CARING TIME   15 min

APPLY THE LESSON AND PRAY FOR ONE ANOTHER

LEADER

Bring the group back together for the Caring Time. Begin by sharing responses to all three questions. Then share prayer requests and close in a group prayer. Those who don't feel comfortable praying out loud should not feel pressured to do so. As the leader, conclude the prayer time and remember to pray for the empty chair.

This time of sharing and prayer is particularly important for the mutual encouragement of the group. Take turns responding to the following questions, and then pray for one another. Pray especially that the Lord will teach you to be more like the "good ground" (v. 20).

1.   What was the best thing that happened to you last week? What was the worst?

2.   How can the group help you to become better "ground"? What prayers do you need regarding your answer to question 6?

3.   Do you have friends or family who need the "seed" of the Gospel "sown" for them? Pray for those people as a group, and invite them to the study next week.

NEXT WEEK

Today we considered Jesus' role as a teacher, and we listened to the parable of the sower. We were reminded that it is not enough just to study God's Word; we also need to allow God's truth to take root and grow in our lives. In the coming week, look at your life for obstacles that might be hindering that growth, and ask the Holy Spirit for help in overcoming those obstacles. Next week we will focus on Jesus as a miraculous healer of our bodies, souls and minds.

NOTES ON MARK 4:1 - 20

Summary: This parable clearly is intended to be a comment upon the four types of responses to Jesus seen in chapter 3, in which the Pharisees accuse him of being demon-possessed (3:22), the crowd seeks him out as a miracle worker to be enjoyed for their purposes (John 6:14,24-26), his family, concerned that things are getting out of hand, thinks he is mad (3:21), and the disciples sit at his feet to listen and practice his teaching (3:34–35).

4:2 *parables.* Parables are comparisons that draw upon common experience in order to teach about the realities of God's kingdom. These metaphors or analogies are often presented in story form; they draw upon the known to explain the unknown. They are often strange or vivid, forcing the hearer to think about their meaning.

4:3 *Listen!* Pay attention! There is more to this story than appears at first. Jesus uses this word to warn the hearers that they must think about this or they will get it wrong. sower *who went out to sow.* Farmers would throw seed into the soil by a broadcast method, indiscriminately throwing seed throughout the entire plot before plowing the ground (including the areas with weeds and a rocky base under shallow soil).

4:4 *the path.* There were long, hard pathways between the various plots of land. The soil of the pathways was so packed down that seed could not penetrate the soil and germinate. The birds came along and ate up this seed that just sat on the surface of the ground.

4:5 *rocky ground.* Some soil covered a limestone base a few inches beneath the surface. Seed that fell here would germinate but it would not last, since a proper root system could not develop because of the rock.

4:7 *thorns.* In other places, there were the roots of weeds. When the seed grew up, so did the weeds, which invariably stunted the growth of the good seed. Although it lived, such seed would not bear fruit.

4:8 *good ground.* However, some of the seed did fall where it could germinate, grow and produce a crop. *30, 60, and 100 times.* The good soil yielded a spectacular crop. The normal yield for a Palestinian field is 7 times what is sown, while 10 times is an especially good harvest. This is where the emphasis in the parable lies: not with the unproductive soil, but with the miracle crop. This is what would have arrested the attention of Jesus' hearers.

4:11 *The secret.* A secret in the New Testament is something which was previously unknown but has now been revealed to all who will hear. The secret given the disciples is that the kingdom of God has come. *the kingdom of God.* How God establishes his reign in human affairs is what Jesus' parables in this section are all about. *has been granted to you.* It is only the spiritual mind that can understand the wisdom of God (1 Cor. 2:10-15). It involves the presence of the Holy Spirit who is a gift from God. It is as the disciples follow Jesus that they will come to understand more fully what he means. *those outside.* The point is not that God calls some and excludes others. Rather, those who are on the outside are simply those who fail to pursue the kingdom. The secret is open to all who, like the disciples, ask.

4:12 *look and look ... listen and listen.* This quotation is from Isaiah 6:9–10, in which God called the prophet to speak his word even though Israel would not listen. Although they saw God's messenger and heard his word, they refused to heed his message. *might turn back—and be forgiven.* It was not that God did not want people to repent as a result of the preaching of Isaiah. This verse can only be understood when one sees it as full of irony, a characteristic of Isaiah's writing. From God's perspective, the behavior of the people is such that it seems the last thing they want to do is actually experience God's forgiveness. Choosing rather to persist in sin, they cover their eyes and block their ears to God's Word so that they will not be persuaded to turn to God. Jesus uses this quotation to indicate that the same thing is happening in his day. Those on the outside are those who refuse to see and hear what he is saying because they do not want to change their ways.

4:15 Some, like the teachers of the Law, are so hardened (like the soil on the paths between plots) that the seed of the Word never penetrates. It is snatched away by Satan before it can germinate. *Satan.* The teachers of the Law have charged Jesus with being dominated by Satan when, in fact, it turns out that they are the ones under his influence!

4:16 *receive it with joy.* Indeed, the common people flocked to Jesus once they saw what he could do (Mark 1:21-45; 3:7–12).

4:19 *the pleasure of wealth, and the desires for other things.* Being a disciple of Christ requires wholehearted loyalty to him. While money and the "other things" in view here are not evil in themselves, the disciple is warned not to allow anything else to take priority over hearing and practicing the words of Jesus. *it becomes unfruitful.* The weeds do not kill the plant (unlike the seed sown on hard ground or on rocky soil, neither of which survive) but they do prevent it from bringing forth fruit.

4:20 But in the end, some, like the Twelve, will reproduce abundantly (3:13–19). These are people who respond to Jesus' word by consistently putting it into practice. *a crop.* The crop in view here is a life full of the qualities of discipleship, such as righteousness, love, joy, peace, goodness, etc. (Gal. 5:22–23; Phil. 1:11).

SESSION 3

HEALER

SCRIPTURE   MATTHEW 9:18–34

Foundations of the Faith

LAST WEEK

JESUS SPENT MUCH OF HIS TIME ON EARTH TEACHING GREAT SPIRITUAL TRUTHS ABOUT THE KINGDOM OF GOD TO THE DISCIPLES AND ALL WHO WOULD LISTEN. WE WERE REMINDED, IN LAST WEEK'S SESSION, THAT GOD EXPECTS US TO BE RECEPTIVE LISTENERS TO JESUS' TEACHINGS, PRODUCING SPIRITUAL FRUIT IN OUR LIVES. THIS WEEK WE WILL FOCUS ON JESUS AS A HEALER, AND LEARN THAT HE PROVIDES SPIRITUAL AND PHYSICAL HEALING FOR THOSE WHO ASK.

ICE-BREAKER

15 min

CONNECT WITH YOUR GROUP

LEADER

Open with a word of prayer, and then welcome and introduce any new members. Choose one, two or all three of the Ice-Breaker questions, depending on your group's needs. Remember to stick to the three-part agenda and the time allowed for each segment.

"If you don't have your health, you don't have anything." While this saying is not completely true, our physical health can have a great impact on all other aspects of our lives. Jesus knew this and took great joy in ministering to the needs of those around him. Take turns sharing some of your thoughts and experiences with sickness and health.

1. If your emotional health this past week could be measured with a thermometer, what would have been your temperature?
    • 98.6—Normal, healthy.
    • 97.5—Turning cold in the midst of stress or frustrations.
    • 99.9—Probably nobody noticed, but I've been a little out of sorts.
    • 102—Things have definitely been heating up inside.
    • 106—The stress is burning my brain, everything is hazy, and I'm not sure how I made it this far!

2. Have you ever had a near-death experience? What happened?

3. Which childhood illnesses have you had?
    • Measles.
    • Mumps.
    • Chicken Pox.
    • Whooping Cough.
    • Other _____.

BIBLE STUDY   30 min

READ SCRIPTURE AND DISCUSS

LEADER

Select a member of the group ahead of time to read aloud the Scripture passage. Then discuss the Questions for Interaction, dividing into subgroups of three to six.

Jesus' ministry flourished despite the opposition that he encountered. While the leaders railed at him for being religiously unorthodox, Jesus simply healed people. In the face of his powerful healings, the words of his critics could not prevail in the hearts and minds of the crowds. Read Matthew 9:18–34, and note the reaction of the Pharisees.

Healing the Sick

[18]As He was telling them these things, suddenly one of the leaders came and knelt down before Him, saying, "My daughter is near death, but come and lay Your hand on her, and she will live." [19]So Jesus and His disciples got up and followed him.

[20]Just then, a woman who had suffered from bleeding for 12 years approached from behind and touched the tassel on His robe, [21]for she said to herself, "If I can just touch His robe, I'll be made well!"

[22]But Jesus turned and saw her. "Have courage, daughter," He said. "Your faith has made you well." And the woman was made well from that moment.

[23]When Jesus came to the leader's house, He saw the flute players and a crowd lamenting loudly. [24]"Leave," He said, "because the girl isn't dead, but sleeping." And they started laughing at Him. [25]But when the crowd had been put outside, He went in and took her by the hand, and the girl got up. [26]And this news spread throughout that whole area.

²⁷As Jesus went on from there, two blind men followed Him, shouting, "Have mercy on us, Son of David!"

²⁸When He entered the house, the blind men approached Him, and Jesus said to them, "Do you believe that I can do this?"

"Yes, Lord," they answered Him.

²⁹Then He touched their eyes, saying, "Let it be done for you according to your faith!" ³⁰And their eyes were opened. Then Jesus warned them sternly, "Be sure that no one finds out!" ³¹But they went out and spread the news about Him throughout that whole area.

³²Just as they were going out, a demon-possessed man who was unable to speak was brought to Him. ³³When the demon had been driven out, the man spoke. And the crowds were amazed, saying, "Nothing like this has ever been seen in Israel!"

³⁴The Pharisees however, said, "He drives out demons by the ruler of the demons!"

Matthew 9:18–34

QUESTIONS FOR INTERACTION

LEADER

Refer to the Summary and Study Notes at the end of this session as needed. If 30 minutes is not enough time to answer all of the questions in this section, conclude the Bible Study by answering question 7.

1. How do you think people today would react if they saw Jesus perform these kinds of miracles?
    • They would follow him.
    • They would believe that there were other explanations for his power.
    • Their hearts would be so hardened from sin that they would reject him.
    • Other _____.

2. What is the social status of the four people that Jesus heals in this passage? Which one took the biggest chance in approaching Jesus?

3. How did the woman (v. 20) obtain healing? The blind men (v. 28)? How did they demonstrate faith?

4.   Who exercised faith in the resurrection of the young girl? Of the demon-possessed man? What action was required of these people?

5.   What things, besides physical illness, can Jesus heal today? What acts of faith might be required?

6.   The following people indicated their faith as they came to Jesus for help. With which person do you most identify?
• Woman suffering from bleeding.
• The leader.
• Two blind men.
• The demon-possessed man.

7.   If Jesus came to you today, for what kind of healing would you ask him?

GOING DEEPER

If your group has time and/or wants a challenge, go on to this question.

8.   The Pharisees accused Jesus of actually serving Satan rather than God. How might we have attitudes similar to that of the Pharisees?

CARING TIME   15 min

APPLY THE LESSON AND PRAY FOR ONE ANOTHER

LEADER

Begin the Caring Time by having group members take turns sharing responses to all three questions. Be sure to save at least the last five minutes for a time of group prayer. Remember to include a prayer for the empty chair when concluding the prayer time.

Foundations of the Faith

Comfort and encourage one another with this time of sharing and prayer. Begin by sharing your responses to the following questions. Be sure to offer any prayer requests and concerns before closing in prayer. Pray especially that the Lord will bring healing in the lives of those around you.

1. Where are you in the journey of following Christ?
   • I am a seeker.
   • I have just begun the journey.
   • I am returning after getting lost on the wrong path.
   • I have been following Christ for a long time.
   • Other _____.

2. How can the group pray for you regarding your answer to question 7?

3. Share the name of someone else, outside of this group, who is in need of healing.

NEXT WEEK

In today's study, we were reminded that Jesus is the Great Physician, the only one who can provide real healing for all areas of a person's life. In the coming week, ask Jesus to begin healing any broken relationships, physical ailments or whatever is causing pain in your life. Next week we will focus on how Jesus handled temptation, and what his example says to us about overcoming sin.

NOTES ON MATTHEW 9:18 – 34

Summary: The four miracles in this passage show Jesus restoring health, life, sight and speech. They are not meant to simply show Jesus' power. They are meant to be pointers to Jesus' identity as the Servant of God who has come to establish the new order of God's kingdom (Isa. 61:1–3). The very nature of his healings provides insights regarding what the kingdom of God will be like when it is fully revealed. It is a realm of restoration and life, free from all types of forces that oppress and destroy.

9:18 *one of the leaders.* Mark and Luke indicate that this man was the ruler of the local synagogue. *knelt down before Him.* In light of the opposition Jesus has received from the official leaders of the people, it could not have been easy for this man, a leader in his community, to humble himself before Jesus in this way. But his concern for his daughter outweighed his pride. *lay Your hand on her.* The laying on of hands was a common practice for ordination, for blessing and for healing.

9:20 *a woman who had suffered from bleeding.* This woman was probably hemorrhaging from the womb. In addition to the obvious physical weakness such a chronic problem would produce, this particular problem rendered her ritually impure or unclean (Lev. 15:25–30). As a result, she was not allowed to take part in temple worship, was unable to have any sexual relations with her husband, and was not supposed to be present in a crowd where others might brush up against her and also become "unclean." The long-term effects of this stigma must have eroded her marriage, her self-concept and her relationship with God.

9:21 *touch His robe.* Somehow, this woman had heard of Jesus' power and took the chance that he might heal her. Perhaps out of fear of rejection because she was "unclean," she did not even dare approach Jesus openly like the ruler. She simply wanted to touch his cloak without drawing any attention to herself at all.

9:22 *Have courage, daughter.* Jesus not only had power to heal her body; his words are intended to heal her spirit as he affirms her as a true child of God. *Your faith has made you well.* It was her faith that impelled her to reach out to Jesus—the source of healing power. Jesus' words point out that there is no magic involved in his healing. It is a matter of God's response to her faith in reaching out to him. The word Jesus uses to tell her that she is healed comes from the same root as the words "salvation" and "Savior." Spiritual as well as physical healing is in view here.

9:23 *flute players and a crowd.* These were in all likelihood professional mourners. Even the poorest person was required to hire not less than two flutes and one wailing woman to mourn a death.

9:24 *the girl isn't dead, but sleeping.* Jesus does not mean by this that she has not really died or is in some sort of coma. The presence of the mourners and the laughter that greeted this statement all say the same thing: the child was truly dead. Jesus uses this same expression in reference to Lazarus, and he was clearly dead. His body had even begun to decompose (John 11:11–15). What he means is that she is not permanently dead.

9:27 *two blind men.* Blindness was common in the ancient world, often due to infection. *Have mercy on us.* Mercy is not as much an emotion as it is concrete aid. *Son of David.* There was a strong expectation that the Messiah would be a king in the line of David. The Messiah was understood to have the power to heal (Matt. 11:4–5). Three of the four times in Matthew where there is an appeal for mercy, the title Son of David is used.

9:29 *according to your faith.* As with the story of the woman (v. 22), faith in Christ is shown to be the key that provides access to God's gracious power. The point is that God delights to respond to those who place their hope in him. But God is not a genie, nor is faith the magic lamp that gets God to do what one wants.

9:33 *Nothing like this has ever been seen in Israel!* At the end of this section of Matthew, Jesus' teaching is contrasted with that of the religious leaders (7:28–29). Here he contrasts his healing power with theirs. The testimony of the crowd to Jesus' miracle working is included.

9:34 The reaction of the Pharisees stands in sharp contrast to the reaction of the crowd in verse 33. The Pharisees dismiss Jesus' healings by attributing them to Satan.

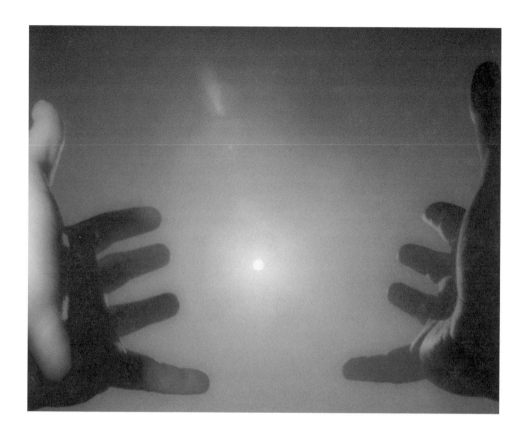

SESSION 4

TEMPTED

SCRIPTURE MATTHEW 4:1-11

Foundations of the Faith

IN LAST WEEK'S SESSION, WE LOOKED AT JESUS' ROLE AS THE GREAT PHYSICIAN,
THE HEALER OF OUR SPIRITUAL, PHYSICAL AND EMOTIONAL NEEDS. WE WERE REMINDED
THAT IN GOD'S KINGDOM THERE IS RESTORATION AND LIFE, AND THAT JESUS'
SACRIFICIAL DEATH PURCHASED THIS ETERNAL LIFE FOR ALL WHO BELIEVE IN HIM.
THIS WEEK WE WILL CONSIDER HOW JESUS DEALT WITH TEMPTATION IN HIS LIFE,
AND SEE HOW HIS EXAMPLE CAN TEACH US HOW TO OVERCOME SIN.

ICE-BREAKER   15 min

CONNECT WITH YOUR GROUP

LEADER

Open the session with a word of prayer, and then welcome and introduce any new group members. Choose one, two or all three of the Ice-Breaker questions.

Jesus experienced temptation just as we do. He was tempted by power and ambition, and by his own physical needs. Take turns sharing your thoughts and experiences with temptation.

1. When you were a teenager, which of the following temptations did you fall into?
    • Driving too fast.
    • Staying out past curfew.
    • Forging my parents' signature.
    • Skipping school.
    • Smoking in the bathroom.
    • Saying hurtful things.
    • Other _____.

2. What is the longest period of time that you've gone without food? What food did you miss the most?

3. If someone gave you $1,000, what would you do with the money?

BIBLE STUDY   30 min

READ SCRIPTURE AND DISCUSS

LEADER

Ask three members of the group, selected ahead of time, to read aloud the Scripture passage. Have one member read the part of Matthew, the narrator; another read the part of Jesus; and the third person the part of Satan. Then discuss the Questions for Interaction, dividing into subgroups of three to six.

Just before Jesus began his public ministry, he was tempted in the desert. His victory over temptation is used as a source of encouragement for the believer. Read Matthew 4:1–11, and note how Jesus uses Scripture to overcome Satan.

The Temptation of Jesus

Matthew: **4** Then Jesus was led up by the Spirit into the wilderness to be tempted by the Devil. ²And after He had fasted 40 days and 40 nights, He was hungry. ³Then the tempter approached Him and said,

Satan: "If You are the Son of God, tell these stones to become bread."

Matthew: ⁴But He answered,

Jesus: "It is written:
'Man must not live on bread alone, but on every word that comes from the mouth of God.'"

Matthew: ⁵Then the Devil took Him to the holy city, had Him stand on the pinnacle of the temple, ⁶and said to Him,

Satan: "If You are the Son of God, throw Yourself down. For it is written:
'He will give His angels orders concerning you, and,
they will support you with their hands,
so that you will not strike your foot against a stone.'"

◆ Foundations of the Faith ◆

Matthew: ⁷Jesus told him,

Jesus: "It is also written:
                  'You must not tempt the Lord your God.'"

Matthew: ⁸Again, the Devil took Him to a very high mountain and showed Him all the
              kingdoms of the world and their splendor. ⁹And he said to Him,

Satan: "I will give You all these things if You will fall down and worship me."

Matthew: ¹⁰Then Jesus told him,

Jesus: "Go away, Satan! For it is written:
                  'You must worship the Lord your God,
                  and you must serve Him only.'"

Matthew: ¹¹Then the Devil left Him, and immediately angels came and began to serve
              Him.

                                                              Matthew 4:1–11

QUESTIONS FOR INTERACTION

LEADER

Refer to the Summary and Study Notes at the end of this session as needed. If 30 minutes is not enough time to answer all of the questions in this section, conclude the Bible Study by answering questions 7 and 8.

1.   Which of the following things tend to tempt you most powerfully?
      • Material things.
      • Overeating.
      • Wasting time.
      • Overworking.
      • Controlling others.
      • Other _____.

2.   Why does the Devil wait for 40 days before tempting Jesus?

3.   It is not a sin to eat bread. What, then, is the temptation in verse 3?

4. What is the temptation that Jesus faces in verse 6? Why does the Devil quote Scripture here?

5. How does Jesus resist each of these temptations?

6. Of the three types of temptations that Jesus faced, which one would you find most difficult to resist?
   • Appetite—food, sex, pleasure.
   • Recognition—success, stardom, applause.
   • Power—authority, control, wealth.

7. When do you find yourself most vulnerable to the tempter?
   • When I'm tired and under stress.
   • When I'm alone or away from home.
   • When I'm discouraged or depressed.
   • When I least expect it.
   • When I let my mind dwell on certain things.
   • I'm never really tempted.
   • Other _____.

8. What has helped you overcome temptation in the past?

GOING DEEPER

If your group has time and/or wants a challenge, go on to this question.

9. Why does the Devil preface the first two temptations with, "If You are the Son of God"?

Foundations of the Faith

CARING TIME

15 min

APPLY THE LESSON AND PRAY FOR ONE ANOTHER

LEADER

Be sure to save at least 15 minutes for this important time. After sharing together from the following questions, end in a time of group prayer.

Gather around each other in this time of sharing and prayer. Pray especially that the Lord will help you as individuals and as a group to grow stronger against temptations.

1.   What areas of temptation are you struggling with at present?

2.   How can the group help you to resist temptations?

3.   Are there ways in which you might be causing someone else to be tempted?

NEXT WEEK

Today we considered how Jesus himself was tempted in the same ways that we are tempted, yet he did not ever fall into sin. We were reminded of the importance of studying Scripture and using the Word of God to resist temptation. In the coming week, ask Jesus to teach you how you can become more like him, using his power to resist the Devil. Next week we will focus on Jesus' role as a revolutionary and his willingness to overcome any power or authority that could get in the way of God's plan.

NOTES ON MATTHEW 4:1 – 11

Summary: Matthew, Mark and Luke all begin the public ministry of Jesus with his baptism and temptation. At his baptism, he is affirmed as God's beloved Son. Through the temptation he is portrayed as the true servant of God. The final temptation has to do with gaining the kingdoms of the world without suffering the coming agonies of the Cross.

4:1 *led up by the Spirit into the wilderness to be tempted.* The same Spirit who had come to Jesus in such affirming power now sends him forth to this time of testing. Jesus' victory over temptation would demonstrate three things: his sinless character; an example of endurance through time of testing; and how to use Scripture as a means of defense against the Devil and a support in the face of evil. ***tempted.*** The nature of the testing he must face has to do with whether or not he would be faithful to his role as the Son of God. ***the Devil.*** Satan does not figure prominently in the Old Testament (although the New Testament identifies the serpent in the Garden of Eden as Satan—Rev. 12:9). But in later Jewish thought and in the New Testament he is portrayed as an angel who has rebelled against God and is set against God's purposes and people (Job 1:6).

4:2 *40 days.* Moses fasted 40 days on Mount Sinai while receiving the commandments (Ex. 34:28), and Israel was in the wilderness 40 years (Deut. 8:2).

4:3 *the tempter approached.* The Spirit led Jesus into the wilderness but it is Satan who tests him. His challenges to Jesus come only after Jesus has entered a condition of physical weakness because of his fast. ***If You are the Son of God.*** This was a temptation to verify the truth of what God had declared (Matt. 3:17). ***bread.*** Satan was asking Jesus to use his supernatural powers for his own ends (hunger). Jesus didn't need to prove to Satan that he was the Son of God. He was able to miraculously provide food, as in the miracle of the loaves and fishes, but it was for God's glory, not to answer Satan.

4:4 Jesus' response is drawn from Deuteronomy 8:3. Originally, this was a reflection on the meaning of the manna in the desert. True life involves not just the physical, but also the spiritual (Word of God). Jesus will not heed Satan, but listens only to his Father.

4:5 *temple.* The second temptation takes place at the temple, which is the focal point in Israel of God's love and power. The challenge is to prove this love and power of God by creating a peril from which God alone can rescue him.

4:6 *If You are the Son of God.* Once again the challenge is to demonstrate that Jesus is the Messiah. ***it is written.*** Satan now quotes Scripture, but does so in a way that tears it from its context. Psalm 91:11–12 are words of assurance to God's people that they can trust God to be with them even through difficult times. Satan twists this to mean that Jesus ought to deliberately put himself in a life-threatening situation to see if God really will bail him out.

4:7 Jesus responds that people are not to test God, as Deuteronomy 6:16 clearly states, but to trust him.

4:9 *I will give You all these things.* Satan offers Jesus a painless, immediate way to power and fame. In fact, by his obedience to the Father, Jesus would become the King of kings, possessing all authority and power (Ps. 2:8; Dan. 7:14).

4:11 *angels came and began to serve Him.* One function of angels is to bring comfort and aid to God's people (Heb. 1:14). Thus prepared by his baptism and his temptation, Jesus begins his ministry.

SESSION 5

REVOLUTIONARY

SCRIPTURE   MARK 2:13–22;   3:1–6

WELCOME

OUR FOCUS IN LAST WEEK'S SESSION WAS ON THE TEMPTATION OF JESUS IN THE WILDERNESS. WE FOUND THAT JESUS CAN HELP US THROUGH TRIALS AND TEMPTATIONS BECAUSE HE WAS ALSO TEMPTED AS WE ARE. WE ALSO SAW HOW THE WORD OF GOD CAN BE A POWERFUL TOOL IN OVERCOMING THE SIN IN OUR LIVES. THIS WEEK WE WILL CONSIDER A DIFFERENT ASPECT OF JESUS' LIFE—THAT OF A REVOLUTIONARY. WE WILL DISCOVER THAT JESUS NEVER LETS THE EXPECTATIONS OF MAN HINDER THE WILL OF GOD.

ICE-BREAKER   15 min

CONNECT WITH YOUR GROUP

LEADER

Open the session with a word of prayer, and then choose one or two of the Ice-Breaker questions. If you have a new group member, you may want to do all three. Remember to stick closely to the three-part agenda and the time allowed for each segment.

Many times, Jesus went against the grain of society. He was often viewed as a radical, as one who didn't hesitate to question the established order. Take turns sharing your "radical" thoughts and experiences.

1. Which of the following choices in each pair would you be more likely to do?

   Go rollerblading _____ Watch TV

   Try exotic foods _____ Eat the usual

   Go skydiving _____ Put together a puzzle

   Spend my inheritance _____ Put money in the bank

   Say what I think _____ Keep my opinions to myself

   Take an African safari _____ Take a vacation close to home

2. What is the most "radical" or "revolutionary" thing you've ever done?

3. If you could change or repeal one law in society, what would it be?

BIBLE STUDY

READ SCRIPTURE AND DISCUSS

30 min

LEADER

Select three members of the group ahead of time to read aloud the Scripture passage. Then discuss the Questions for Interaction, dividing into subgroups of three to six.

The greatest opposition to Jesus came from religious leaders. In the three stories that follow, we see them probe and question Jesus. Then they come to the conclusion that not only is Jesus dangerous, but he must be killed. Read Mark 2:13–22; 3:1–6, and note how Jesus always puts people's needs before rules and regulations.

Lord of the Sabbath

Reader One: ¹³Then Jesus went out again beside the sea. The whole crowd was coming to Him, and He taught them. ¹⁴Then, moving on, He saw Levi the son of Alphaeus sitting at the tax office, and He said to him, "Follow Me!" So he got up and followed Him.

¹⁵While He was reclining at the table in Levi's house, many tax collectors and sinners were also guests with Jesus and His disciples, because there were many who were following Him. ¹⁶When the scribes of the Pharisees saw that He was eating with sinners and tax collectors, they asked His disciples, "Why does He eat with tax collectors and sinners?"

¹⁷When Jesus heard this, He told them, "Those who are well don't need a doctor, but the sick do need one. I didn't come to call the righteous, but sinners."

Reader Two: ¹⁸Now John's disciples and the Pharisees were fasting. People came and asked Him, "Why do John's disciples and the Pharisees' disciples fast, but Your disciples do not fast?"

¹⁹Jesus said to them, "The wedding guests cannot fast while the groom is with them, can they? As long as they have the groom with them, they cannot fast. ²⁰But the time will come when the groom is taken away from them, and then they will fast in that day. ²¹No one sews a patch of unshrunk cloth on an old garment. Otherwise, the new patch pulls away

from the old cloth, and a worse tear is made. ²²And no one puts new wine into old wineskins. Otherwise, the wine will burst the skins, and the wine is lost as well as the skins. But new wine is for fresh wineskins."...

Reader Three: **3** Now He entered the synagogue again, and a man was there who had a paralyzed hand. ²In order to accuse Him, the Pharisees were watching Him closely to see whether He would heal him on the Sabbath. ³He told the man with the paralyzed hand, "Stand before us." ⁴Then He said to them, "Is it lawful on the Sabbath to do good or to do evil, to save life or to kill?" But they were silent. ⁵After looking around at them with anger and sorrow at the hardness of their hearts, He told the man, "Stretch out your hand." So he stretched it out, and his hand was restored. ⁶Immediately the Pharisees went out and started plotting with the Herodians against Him, how they might destroy Him.

Mark 2:13–22; 3:1–6

QUESTIONS FOR INTERACTION

LEADER

Refer to the Summary and Study Notes at the end of this session as needed. If 30 minutes is not enough time to answer all of the following questions in this section, conclude the Bible Study by answering question 7.

1. Levi immediately responded to following Jesus. What has drawn you to Jesus?
    • His love.
    • His compassion.
    • His countercultural values.
    • The example of his love I've seen in others.
    • A sense of obligation.
    • My parents' teachings.
    • I'm not really sure.
    • Other _____.

2. Tax collectors, such as Levi, were renowned for cheating and greedy dishonesty, yet Jesus asks Levi to become a disciple (2:14). What does this teach us about Jesus? About Levi?

3.   What does Jesus mean in 2:17, "I didn't come to call the righteous, but sinners"? Who are the "righteous" to whom Jesus is referring? Who are the "sinners"?

4.   What is the lesson that Jesus is teaching in his analogies of patched garments and wineskins? (See notes for more information.)

5.   Why did Jesus heal the man on the Sabbath?
     • Because there was no reason to wait until the next day.
     • To spite the Pharisees.
     • Because he had compassion on the man.
     • To demonstrate that he was Lord of the Sabbath.
     • Other _____.

6.   What did Jesus say about the rules the Pharisees followed on the Sabbath (3:4)? What changes do you need to make regarding the way you observe your Sabbath?

7.   How have you seen religious rules cause people to focus on the wrong things? How might you be guilty of distracting others from following God?

GOING DEEPER

If your group has time and/or wants a challenge, go on to this question.

8.   The guests at Levi's dinner party (2:15) were probably his friends and associates. What do we learn from this party about Jesus? About Levi?

CARING TIME

15 min

APPLY THE LESSON AND PRAY FOR ONE ANOTHER

LEADER

Be sure everyone is receiving prayer support during this important time. After sharing together from the following questions, end in a time of group prayer.

Come together once again for a time of sharing and prayer. Pray especially that the Lord might help you as a group and as individuals to see areas where rules or habits are interfering with God's work.

1. How is your relationship with Jesus right now?
    - Close.
    - Improving.
    - Growing apart.
    - Distant.
    - Strained.
    - Other _____.

2. How can we work as a group to draw one another closer to Jesus?

3. What issues with your church or your lifestyle are coming between you and Jesus?

NEXT WEEK

Today we saw how the Pharisees looked at Jesus as a revolutionary and radical. We were encouraged by Jesus' example to be bold when necessary and break through the man-made rules and expectations of our culture. In the coming week, examine your life, your church and your whole environment to consider whether you might have patterns that are hindering the Lord's work. Next week we will focus on Jesus as our Redeemer. We will learn that Jesus did not let anything, not even his own life, stand in the way of God's redemptive work for mankind.

NOTES ON MARK 2:13 — 22; 3:1 — 6

Summary: Mark tells these three stories in order to show the nature of (and reason for) the opposition of Jesus by the religious leaders. They are set in contrast to a previous series of stories (1:16–45) that show how popular Jesus was with the common people. News about Jesus has spread everywhere (1:28,45). It is not surprising, therefore, that the religious leaders want to know who he is and what he stands for.

2:14 *Levi.* Elsewhere he is identified as Matthew (Matt. 9:9), the disciple who eventually wrote one of the Gospels. In his role as a tax collector, both the religious establishment and the common people would have hated Matthew. Jews in this business were seen as traitors to Israel, financially profiting through exploiting their own people by cooperating with the Roman oppressors. Tax collectors were considered as vile as robbers or murderers. For Jesus to associate with Levi and his friends would raise the same objections most church people today would feel if they knew their pastor was associating closely with Mafia figures. *Follow Me.* In Matthew, Mark and Luke, this is the key phrase regarding discipleship. Only those who leave their past behind to follow Jesus in faith and obedience are his disciples. While we are not told what else transpired that moved Matthew to respond this way, the crucial point is that he did choose to turn away from his past loyalties to pursue the way of Jesus.

2:15 *reclining at the table.* People in Jesus' time ate meals while sitting in a reclining position. To share a meal with another was a significant event, implying acceptance of that person. In this way, Jesus extends his forgiveness (v. 15) to those who were outside orthodox religious life.

2:16 *Pharisees.* This was a small, strict sect of Jews who devoted themselves to observing the traditions of the rabbis as a means of gaining God's favor. Seeing themselves as the truly righteous in Israel, they tended as a whole to look down upon other Jews who could not follow their practices.

2:19 *the groom.* In the Old Testament, God was often referred to as Israel's bridegroom, another subtle indication of Jesus' divine identity.

2:20 *is taken away from them.* An ominous note predicting Jesus' death. That would be an appropriate time for fasting as a genuine expression of his disciples' grief for sin and desire for God's mercy.

2:22 *new wine.* New wine is still fermenting. Hence, no one would have poured it into a leather container that was old, dry and crusty. New wine required new skins that were supple and flexible, able to expand as the wine fermented. Otherwise, the fermenting wine would burst the skin, ruining the skin and spilling the wine.

3:2 *watching Him closely.* By this time the religious leaders no longer questioned Jesus. Now they simply watched to see if his actions betrayed a disregard for the Law so they might accuse him. ***whether He would heal him on the Sabbath.*** The issue is not healing, but whether Jesus would do so on the Sabbath in defiance of the oral tradition, which allowed healing only if there was danger to life. Jesus could have waited until the next day to heal this long-paralyzed hand. These Pharisees fail to see the need of the man, focusing only on the mandates of their tradition.

3:3 *Stand before us.* As with the paralytic, Jesus once again takes a deliberate action to force the confrontation with his questioners. He did not shy away from their accusations, but took action to expose the foolishness of the charges of his opponents.

3:4 *Then He said to them.* Jesus' implication is that refusing to heal this man just because it was the Sabbath was actually to commit evil, since a real human need would be allowed to go unmet. ***they were silent.*** Their silence reflected their refusal to reconsider their position.

3:5 *anger and sorrow.* Jesus felt strongly about the injustice of a system that sacrificed the genuine needs of people for religious traditions that had nothing to do with God. ***Stretch out your hand.*** Just as he deliberately declared the paralytic's sins forgiven (knowing that this was blasphemy to the teachers of the Law), here he deliberately heals on the Sabbath (knowing that this too was anathema to his critics).

3:6 *Herodians.* A political group made up of influential Jewish sympathizers of King Herod. They were normally despised by the Pharisees, who considered them traitors (for working with Rome) and irreligious (unclean as a result of their association with Gentiles). ***how they might destroy Him.*** Mark makes use of irony here. The Pharisees believed Jesus violated the Sabbath by healing on that day, but failed to see that they themselves were violating the Sabbath law by plotting how to kill him on that day!

SESSION 6

REDEEMER

SCRIPTURE MARK 14:12 – 26

LAST WEEK

JESUS WAS CONSIDERED A RADICAL AND REVOLUTIONARY BY THE ESTABLISHED RELIGIOUS AUTHORITIES, AS WE SAW IN OUR SESSION LAST WEEK. WE ALSO SAW THAT JESUS WAS NOT AFRAID TO CONFRONT THE TRADITIONS AND INSTITUTIONS OF MAN WHEN THEY OPPOSED THE REDEMPTIVE WORK OF GOD. THIS WEEK WE WILL FOCUS ON JESUS' ROLE AS REDEEMER, AND WE WILL LEARN THE COST THAT JESUS HIMSELF WOULD PAY FOR THAT REDEMPTION.

ICE-BREAKER

15 min

CONNECT WITH YOUR GROUP

LEADER

Begin the session with a word of prayer, asking God for his blessing and presence. Choose one, two or all three Ice-Breaker questions, depending on your group's needs.

From the beginning of time, God had one purpose for his Son—to die on a cross for the sins of the world. The death and resurrection of Jesus Christ is the central doctrine of the Christian faith, and Jesus gave us a way to remember and celebrate that event—he gave us the Lord's Supper. Take turns sharing your unique experiences with remembering special events.

1. What is your favorite holiday meal?
    - Turkey.
    - Lamb.
    - Vegetarian.
    - Chicken.
    - Ham.
    - Other _____.

2. What was the most memorable banquet or party you ever attended?

3. What is your favorite anniversary or memorial holiday?
    - Wedding anniversary.
    - Christmas.
    - Fourth of July.
    - Birthday.
    - Other _____.

BIBLE STUDY

30 min

READ SCRIPTURE AND DISCUSS

LEADER

Ask two group members, selected ahead of time, to read aloud the parts of Mark and Jesus in the Scripture passage. Have the rest of the group read the part of the disciples. Then discuss the Questions for Interaction, dividing into subgroups of three to six.

This scene introduces the Lord's Supper. Instructions for Jesus' arrest had already been issued. However, Jews were required to eat the Passover meal in Jerusalem itself, so Jesus makes secret arrangements to meet with his disciples for their last meal together. He then transforms the Passover's remembrance of God's deliverance of Israel from Egypt into a time of remembering God's deliverance of humanity from sin. Read Mark 14:12–26, and note how Jesus anticipates his role as Redeemer.

The Lord's Supper

Mark: ¹²On the first day of Unleavened Bread, when they sacrifice the Passover lamb, His disciples asked Him,

Disciples: "Where do You want us to go and prepare the Passover so You may eat it?"

Mark: ¹³So He sent two of His disciples and told them,

Jesus: "Go into the city, and a man carrying a water jug will meet you. Follow him. ¹⁴Wherever he enters, tell the owner of the house, 'The Teacher says, "Where is the guest room for Me to eat the Passover with My disciples?" ' ¹⁵He will show you a large room upstairs, furnished and ready. Make the preparations for us there."

Mark: ¹⁶So the disciples went out, entered the city, and found it just as He had told them, and they prepared the Passover. ¹⁷When evening came, He arrived with the Twelve. ¹⁸While they were reclining and eating, Jesus said,

Jesus: "I assure you: One of you will betray Me—one who is eating with Me!"

Mark: [19]They began to be distressed and to say to Him one by one,

Disciples: "Surely not I?"

Mark: [20]He said to them,

Jesus: "It is one of the Twelve—the one who is dipping bread with Me in the bowl. [21]For the Son of Man will go just as it is written about Him, but woe to that man by whom the Son of Man is betrayed! It would have been better for that man if he had not been born."

Mark: [22]As they were eating, He took bread, blessed and broke it, gave it to them, and said,

Jesus: "Take it; this is My body."

Mark: [23]Then He took a cup, and after giving thanks, He gave it to them, and so they all drank from it. [24]He said to them,

Jesus: "This is My blood of the covenant, which is shed for many. [25]I assure you: I will no longer drink of the fruit of the vine until that day when I drink it new in the kingdom of God."

Mark: [26]After singing psalms, they went out to the Mount of Olives.

Mark 14:12–26

QUESTIONS FOR INTERACTION

LEADER

Refer to the Summary and Study Notes at the end of this session as needed. If 30 minutes is not enough time to answer all of the following questions in this section, conclude the Bible Study by answering questions 6 and 7.

1. How do you imagine Jesus felt at this "last supper"?
    • Nostalgic.   • Sad.
    • Relaxed   • Other _____.
    • Anxious to get things over with.

2. Passover was a celebration of God's grace and mercy when the Israelites were about to leave the slavery of Egypt. What do you think are the parallels between Passover and the meaning of the Last Supper?

3. Why is it so significant that Judas, Jesus' betrayer, is eating at the table with him during Passover?

4. What do we discover about the disciples by their reaction to Jesus' statement (vv. 18–19)? How would you have reacted?

5. How did Judas betray Jesus? How might someone today betray Jesus?

6. When did the Lord's Supper take on a personal meaning to you?

7. If we aren't careful, rituals such as the Lord's Supper can lose their significance and become mundane or impersonal. What could you do in preparing for the Lord's Supper to make it more significant to you?

GOING DEEPER

If your group has time and/or wants a challenge, go on to this question.

8. Why does Jesus use bread to symbolize his body? Why wine for his blood?

CARING TIME   15 min

APPLY THE LESSON AND PRAY FOR ONE ANOTHER

LEADER

ollowing the Caring Time, discuss with your group how they would like to celebrate the last session
Following the Caring Time, discuss with your group how they would like to celebrate the last session next week. Also, discuss the possibility of splitting into two groups or continuing together with another study. Consider celebrating the Lord's Supper together as a group.

Foundations of the Faith

Spend some time now encouraging one another and praying for one another. Pray especially that the Lord will bring each of you into a deeper understanding of his sacrificial love.

1. How would you like to thank Jesus for being your Redeemer and bringing you the gift of eternal life?

2. Do you feel that you have ever betrayed Jesus? How can the group help you find forgiveness and peace?

3. Through both Passover and Christ's death, God brought freedom. What do you need to be free from?

NEXT WEEK

Today we have seen that Jesus paid for the redemption of humanity with the ultimate sacrifice, even offering his grace to the one who would betray him. In the coming week, spend time preparing for the Lord's Supper, then celebrate it at church or with the group. Next week, in our final session, we will focus on Jesus, the Reconciler. We will consider how Jesus specializes in reconciliation among all people, no matter how tall or wide the barriers are.

NOTES ON MARK 14:12 – 26

Summary: Through this meal, Jesus formally introduced that his death was the means by which a new covenant was to be established between God and his people. It is this meal that declares Jesus' abiding presence with his people and gives meaning to Jesus' death as a sacrifice for sins. Just as at Passover, a lamb was sacrificed as a means of atoning for the sins of the people, so Jesus' death is a sacrifice which leads God to "pass over" (or forgive) the sins of those who entrust themselves to him.

14:12 ***On the first day of Unleavened Bread.*** The Feast of Unleavened Bread did not officially start until the day after the Passover. However, in the first century, the day on which the lambs were sacrificed was sometimes referred to as the first day of the Feast of Unleavened Bread. ***prepare the Passover.*** The disciples have to set out the unleavened bread and the wine; collect the bitter herbs (horseradish, chicory, etc.); make the sauce in which the bread was dipped (a stew of dried fruit, spices and wine); and roast the lamb on an open fire. The meal began with a blessing and the first of four cups of wine. Psalms were then sung and the story of the deliverance read, followed by the second cup of wine and the eating of the bread, herbs and the sauce (into which Judas and the others dip their bread—see v. 20). Then the meal of roast lamb and bread is eaten. More prayers are said and the third cup is consumed. More psalms are sung; the final cup is drunk, after which a psalm is sung. Two short prayers end the feast.

14:13 *a man carrying a water jug.* Such a person would have been easy to spot and follow, since it was highly unusual for a man to carry a jug. Women carried jugs; men carried wineskins.

14:17 *When evening came.* The Passover meal could be eaten only after sunset. It was a night of excited watching in which people asked: "Will this be the night when God comes again to deliver his people from bondage?"

14:18 *reclining and eating.* People would eat festive meals by lying on couches or cushions arranged around a low table.

14:20 *dipping bread with Me in the bowl.* To share in a meal was a sign of friendship, accenting the act of betrayal.

14:21 *as it is written about Him.* Passages such as Isaiah 53:1–6 point to the suffering of God's chosen servant. *woe to that man.* While the suffering of God's Messiah is part of God's plan, the people involved in that act are responsible for their decisions. *if he had not been born.* This is a stern warning of the judgment to come upon Judas (and others) who turn their backs on Jesus.

14:22 *He took bread, blessed and broke it, and gave it to them.* Commonly at Passover, bread was broken and distributed prior to the meal as a reminder of how God had provided bread for his people in the wilderness. Jesus' action at this point in the meal would be unusual, calling attention to its new, special meaning. *this is My body.* Literally, "This, My body." While the bread used to represent God's provision of food for his people while they wandered in the wilderness, now it is to represent Jesus' body that was broken and torn upon the cross. To share in this bread is to affirm that one finds life in Jesus' sacrifice, is committed to his teaching, and shares in his mission.

14:23 *cup.* Jesus relates the Passover cup of red wine to the renewal of the covenant of God with his people through his sacrificial death.

14:24 *covenant.* It refers to the arrangement that God made with Israel (Ex. 24:1–8), which was dependent on Israel's obedience. Now (as anticipated in Jer. 31:31–33) a new covenant is established, which is made dependent on Jesus' obedience (his sacrificial death). A covenant of law becomes a covenant of love. *shed.* Blood that was poured out symbolized a violent death (Gen. 4:10–11; Deut. 19:10; Matt. 23:35). This phrase points to the type of death Jesus would have. *for many.* This is an idiomatic expression meaning all people (10:45). The point is not that each and every individual will experience the benefits of the covenant regardless of their commitments, but that this is a covenant promise for all types of people throughout the world, not only for the Jews.

14:25 *I will no longer drink.* This may mean that Jesus chose to abstain from the fourth Passover cup which was passed around at the close of the meal, indicating that this Passover meal will only be consummated when Jesus ushers in God's kingdom in its fullness. *the kingdom of God.* The presence of God's reign was often pictured as a great banquet.

SESSION 7

RECONCILER

SCRIPTURE   EPHESIANS 2:11–22

Foundations of the Faith

LAST WEEK

IN LAST WEEK'S SESSION, WE SAT WITH THE LORD AT THE LAST SUPPER, AND CONSIDERED THE PRICE THAT HE PAID TO BRING RECONCILIATION TO HUMANITY. WE ALSO DISCUSSED HOW WE MIGHT PREPARE FOR THE LORD'S SUPPER IN ORDER TO MAKE IT AS MEANINGFUL AS POSSIBLE. IN TODAY'S FINAL SESSION, WE WILL FOCUS ON JESUS AS THE RECONCILER AND HOW HE MAKES RECONCILIATION AVAILABLE FREELY TO ALL PEOPLE WITHOUT ANY FAVORITISM.

ICE-BREAKER

15 min

CONNECT WITH YOUR GROUP

LEADER

Begin this final session with a word of prayer and thanksgiving for this time together. Be sure to affirm each group member for the blessings and contributions that he or she made to the group.

We have studied the life of Jesus as the Messiah, a teacher, a healer, one who was tempted, a revolutionary and a redeemer. As our Redeemer, Jesus broke down the barrier of sin that separated us from God; yet Jesus' life was also an example of breaking down other barriers and being reconciled to all people. Take turns sharing your thoughts and experiences with being reconciled with others.

1. When you were growing up, with what kind of people were you warned not to associate?
    • People of a different national heritage.
    • People who used foul language.
    • People who didn't go to church.
    • People from "the other side of the tracks."
    • People of a different political persuasion.
    • We could associate with anyone.
    • People of another religion.
    • Other _____.

2.   If you grew up in a "blended family," what was it like? How did your family members work at becoming one family unit?

3.   Have you ever been excluded from joining a group? How did it affect you?

| BIBLE STUDY | 30 min |

READ SCRIPTURE AND DISCUSS

LEADER

Ask one group member, selected ahead of time, to read aloud the Scripture passage. Then discuss the Questions for Interaction, dividing into subgroups of three to six. Be sure to save some extra time at the end for the Caring Time.

The work of Christ at the Cross brought reconciliation, not just to Israel, but also to the entire human race. In this selection from Paul's epistle to the Ephesians, the author explains the great riches that have been made available to all people, Jew and Gentile alike. Read Ephesians 2:11–22, and note the hope that Christ brings to us.

One in Christ

[11]So then, remember that at one time you were Gentiles in the flesh—called "the uncircumcised" by those called "the circumcised," done by hand in the flesh. [12]At that time you were without the Messiah, excluded from the citizenship of Israel, and foreigners to the covenants of the promise, with no hope and without God in the world. [13]But now in Christ Jesus, you who were far away have been brought near by the blood of the Messiah. [14]For He is our peace, who made both groups one and tore down the dividing wall of hostility. In His flesh, [15]He did away with the law of the commandments in regulations, so that He might create in Himself one new man from the two, resulting in peace. [16]He did this so that He might reconcile both to God in one body through the cross and put the hostility to death by it. [17]When Christ came, He proclaimed the good news of peace to you who were far away and peace to those who were near. [18]For through Him we both have access by one

Spirit to the Father. ¹⁹So then you are no longer foreigners and strangers, but fellow citizens with the saints, and members of God's household, ²⁰built on the foundation of the apostles and prophets, with Christ Jesus Himself as the cornerstone. ²¹The whole building is being fitted together in Him and is growing into a holy sanctuary in the Lord, ²²in whom you also are being built together for God's dwelling in the Spirit.

Ephesians 2:11–22

QUESTIONS FOR INTERACTION

LEADER

Refer to the Summary and Study Notes at the end of this session as needed. If 30 minutes is not enough time to answer all of the questions in this section, conclude the Bible Study by answering questions 6 and 7.

1. What hopes do you have for your future? What hopes do you have for your church?

2. Paul states that non-Jews had "no hope" prior to Jesus (v. 12). How did Jesus bring this hope to all nations and races?

3. What was the "dividing wall of hostility" (v. 14) that Jesus tore down?

4. What does it mean to be a member of God's household?

5. If we are "being built together for God's dwelling" (v. 22) as believers in Christ, what should be our attitude toward people who are very different from us?

6. What dividing wall would you especially like to break down with God's help, so that we can live in a better world?
   • Strife among different ethnic peoples.
   • Division between rich and poor.
   • National hostilities.
   • Strife between the sexes.
   • Other _____.

7.   How would a person of another background or color be accepted in your group or church?

GOING DEEPER

If your group has time and/or wants a challenge, go on to this question.

8.   What "hostility" has been put to death on the cross? What implication does this have for Christians today?

CARING TIME   15 min

APPLY THE LESSON AND PRAY FOR ONE ANOTHER

LEADER

Conclude this final Caring Time by praying for each group member and asking for God's guidance and blessing in any plans to start a new group or continue to study together.

Gather around each other now in this final time of sharing and prayer, being confident that God will give each of you the strength, wisdom and grace to grow in your relationship and knowledge of Jesus Christ.

1.   How has this group been a blessing in your life?

2.   What are some specific areas in which you have grown in this study about Jesus?
   • In my understanding of who Jesus is.
   • In deepening my relationship and walk with Christ.
   • In submitting to the teachings of Christ.
   • In longing for experiencing more of Jesus as healer.
   • In gaining greater appreciation for Jesus as a revolutionary, redeemer and reconciler.
   • In being stretched to share my faith in Christ more.
   • Other _____.

3.   What relationship in your own life has some walls that God needs to knock down?

NOTES ON EPHESIANS 2:11 - 22

Summary: Paul moves from the problem of human alienation from God (2:1–10) to the related problem of alienation between people themselves (2:11–22). In both cases, the problem is hostility (or enmity). Christ is the one who, through his death, brings peace. First between God and people, but then, also, between human enemies. The particular focus of this section is on the deep hostility between Jew and Gentile.

2:11 *remember.* In 2:1–3, Paul reminded his Gentile readers that once they were trapped in their transgressions and sins, and so were spiritually dead and alienated from God. Here in verse 11, he asks them to remember that once they were also isolated from all the blessings of God. In 2:1–3, the focus is on being cut off from God himself; while in verses 11–13, the focus is on being cut off from God's kingdom and God's people. *the uncircumcised.* This is a derogatory slur by which Gentiles were mocked. With this contemptuous nickname, Jews were saying that the Gentiles' lack of "God's mark" on their bodies put them absolutely outside of God's kingdom, so they were to be despised. *the circumcised.* This is how Jews thought of themselves, and was a term used with pride. Circumcision was the sign given to Abraham by which the covenant people were to be marked. This made the Jew different and special.

2:12 *without the Messiah.* In contrast to the great blessings that come as a result of being "in Christ," at one time the Gentiles were outside Christ. That is, they had no hope of a coming Messiah who would make all things right. Instead, they considered themselves to be caught up in the deadly cycle of history, which led nowhere. The separation from the hope of a Messiah was the first liability faced by the Gentiles. *excluded from the citizenship.* Gentiles were not part of God's kingdom. Israel was a nation founded by God, consisting of his people, and Gentiles were outside that reality. This was their second liability. *foreigners to the covenants.* Not only did Gentiles have no part in God's kingdom, they also stood outside all the amazing agreements (covenants) God made with his people (Ex. 6:4–8; Deut. 28:9–14). This is the third liability. *with no hope.* During this particular historical era, the Roman world experienced a profound loss of hope. The first century was inundated with mystery cults, all promising salvation from this despair. Living in fear of demons, people felt themselves to be mere playthings of the capricious gods. This lack of hope in the face of fear was the fourth liability. *without God.* This is not to say that Gentiles were atheists (even though the word used here is atheos). On the contrary, they worshiped scores of deities. The problem was that they had no effective knowledge of the one true God. This is the final liability.

2:13 *But now.* This is the second great "But," which signals God's intervention into a seemingly hopeless situation. The first use of "But" in this fashion is found in 2:4, where Paul describes what God has done in the face of universal sin and bondage. ***by the blood of the Messiah.*** Paul pinpoints how this great change occurred. It is as a result of Jesus' death on the cross that union with Christ is possible (1:7).

2:14 *our peace.* Jesus brings peace; that is, he creates harmony between people and God. He also creates harmony between individuals and groups. He draws together those who consider each other to be enemies. He does this by being the one who stands between the alienated parties, bridging the gap that separates them. ***the dividing wall of hostility.*** In the temple in Jerusalem an actual wall was built on an elevated area. The Court of the Priests surrounded the inner sanctuary. Beyond this was the Court of Israel (for men only) and then the Court of the Women. All these courts were on the same level as the temple; and each had a different degree of exclusivity. Ringing all the courts and some 19 steps below was the Court of the Gentiles. Here Gentiles could gaze up at the temple. But they could not approach it. They were cut off by a stone wall ("the dividing wall"), bearing signs that warned in Greek and Latin that trespassing foreigners would be killed. Paul himself knew well this prohibition. He had nearly been lynched by a mob of Jews who were told he had taken a Gentile into the temple. ***hostility.*** The ancient world abounded in hostility. There was enmity between Jew and Gentile, Greek and barbarian, men and women, slave and free. Christ ends each form of hostility (Gal. 3;28; Col.3:11).

2:15 *the law of the commandments in regulations.* The primary reference is to the thousands of rules and regulations that were in existence at the time of Christ, by which Jewish leaders sought to define the "Law of Moses" (the first five books of the Old Testament). The belief was that only by keeping all these rules could one be counted "good," and therefore have fellowship with God. ***one new man.*** In the place of divided humanity, Jesus creates a whole new quality of being—a new humanity, as it were. This does not mean that Jews became Gentiles, or that Gentiles became Jews. Both became Christians, "the third race."

2:16 *reconcile.* This word means, "to bring together estranged parties." In verse 14 the emphasis is on reconciling Jew to Gentile. Here the reference is to bringing both Jew and Gentile together with God.

2:17 *He proclaimed the good news of peace.* Since such peace was possible only through the Cross, this reference is probably to Jesus' post-resurrection appearances. His first words to the stunned apostles after his resurrection were, in fact, "Peace be with you!" (John 20:19).

2:18 *access.* In Greek, one form of this word is used to describe an individual whose job it is to usher a person into the presence of the king. Indeed, not only did Jesus open the way back to God (by his death, humanity was reconciled to God), he continues to provide the means whereby an ongoing and continuing relationshipß is possible.

2:19 *foreigners and strangers.* Nonresident aliens who were disliked by the native population and often held in suspicion. *fellow citizens.* Whereas once the Gentiles were "excluded from the citizenship of Israel" (v. 12), now they are members of God's kingdom. They now "belong." *members of God's household.* In fact, their relationship is far more intimate. They have become family.

2:20 *the foundation of the apostles and prophets.* Since both apostles and prophets are teachers, this phrase could mean that the church rests on the teaching of both the Old Testament (prophets) and the New Testament (apostles). However, since the order is reversed, it probably means that the church rests on the teaching of the apostles and the New Testament prophets who followed them. *cornerstone.* That stone which rested firmly on the foundation and tied two walls together, giving each its correct alignment. The temple in Jerusalem had massive cornerstones (one was nearly 40 feet long). The image might be of Jesus holding together Jew and Gentile, Old Testament and New Testament.

2:21 *fitted together.* Used by a mason to describe how two stones were prepared so that they would bond tightly together. *holy sanctuary.* The new temple is not like the old one, carved out of dead stone—beautiful, but forbidding and exclusive. Rather, it is alive all over the world, inclusive of all, and made up of the individuals in whom God dwells.

PERSONAL NOTES

PERSONAL NOTES